Dear Parent:

Your child's love of ▮

Every child learns to read in a d▮▮▮▮▮▮▮ ▮▮ ▮▮▮ ▮▮ her own speed. Some go back and forth b▮▮▮▮▮n reading levels and read favorite books again and again. Others read through each level in order. You can help your young reader improve and become more confident by encouraging his or her own interests and abilities. From books your child reads with you to the first books he or she reads alone, there are I Can Read Books for every stage of reading:

SHARED READING
Basic language, word repetition, and whimsical illustrations, ideal for sharing with your emergent reader

BEGINNING READING
Short sentences, familiar words, and simple concepts for children eager to read on their own

READING WITH HELP
Engaging stories, longer sentences, and language play for developing readers

READING ALONE
Complex plots, challenging vocabulary, and high-interest topics for the independent reader

I Can Read Books have introduced children to the joy of reading since 1957. Featuring award-winning authors and illustrators and a fabulous cast of beloved characters, I Can Read Books set the standard for beginning readers.

A lifetime of discovery begins with the magical words **"I Can Read!"**

Visit www.icanread.com for information
on enriching your child's reading experience.

Visit www.zonderkidz.com/icanread for more faith-based
I Can Read! titles from Zonderkidz.

They trusted in him and defied the king's command
and were willing to give up their lives
rather than serve or worship any god
except their own God.
— *Daniel 3:28*

ZONDERKIDZ

Facing the Blazing Furnace
Copyright © 2015 by Zondervan
Illustrations © 2015 by David Miles

An **I Can Read Book**

Published in Grand Rapids, Michigan, by Zonderkidz. Zonderkidz is a registered
trademark of The Zondervan Corporation, L.L.C., a wholly owned subsidiary of
HarperCollins Christian Publishing, Inc.

Requests for information should be addressed to
customercare@harpercollins.com.

ISBN 978-0-310-75093-2

Editor: Mary Hassinger
Art direction: Deborah Washburn

Printed in Thailand

24 25 26 27 28 /DSC / 21 20 19 18 17 16 15 14 13 12 11 10 9 8 7

Adventure
BIBLE

Facing the Blazing Furnace

Pictures by David Miles

ZONDERkidz
.com

The people of God

lived in the kingdom of Israel.

They were called Jews.

Some of the Jews listened to God.

They followed his commandments.

But some did not.

Some of the Jews

worshiped other gods.

One day, the king of Babylon

attacked the biggest city in Israel!

Their king had a funny name.

His name was Nebuchadnezzar.

His army captured the city

called Jerusalem.

Many Jews were taken to Babylon.

It was a sad day for the Jews.

King Nebuchadnezzar said,
"I want some of the Jewish men
to work for me."

He chose strong, handsome,

and smart men.

They would be trained for three years.

Then they would work for the king.

Four of these young men
were extra special.
Their names were Daniel,
Shadrach, Meshach, and Abednego.

Daniel, Shadrach, Meshach,

and Abednego loved God.

God gave them wisdom.

He made them smart and faithful.

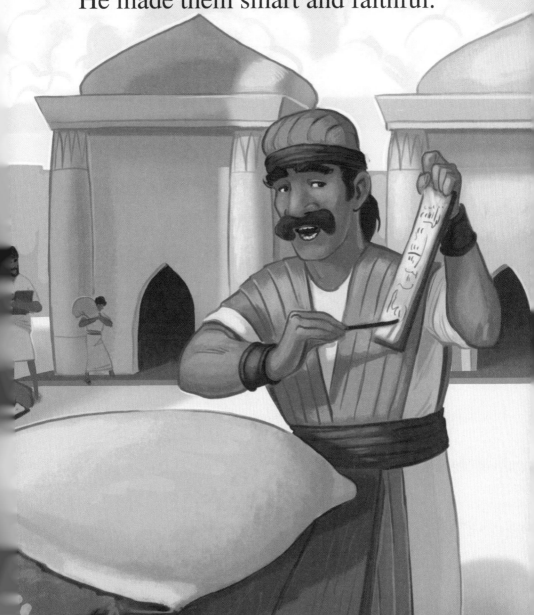

King Nebuchadnezzar
put the young men right to work.

King Nebuchadnezzar

was very happy.

They were ten times smarter

than all the other people

who worked for the king.

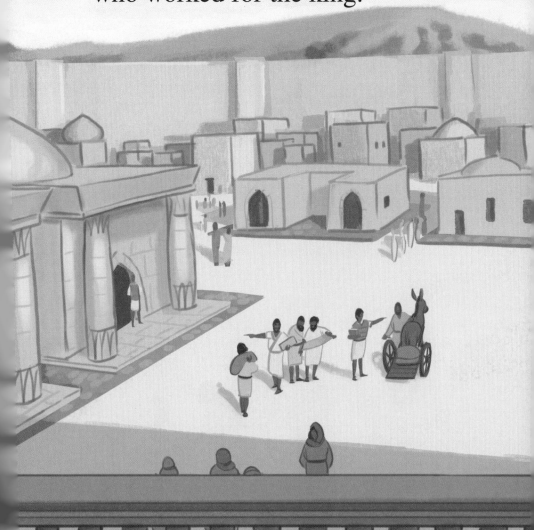

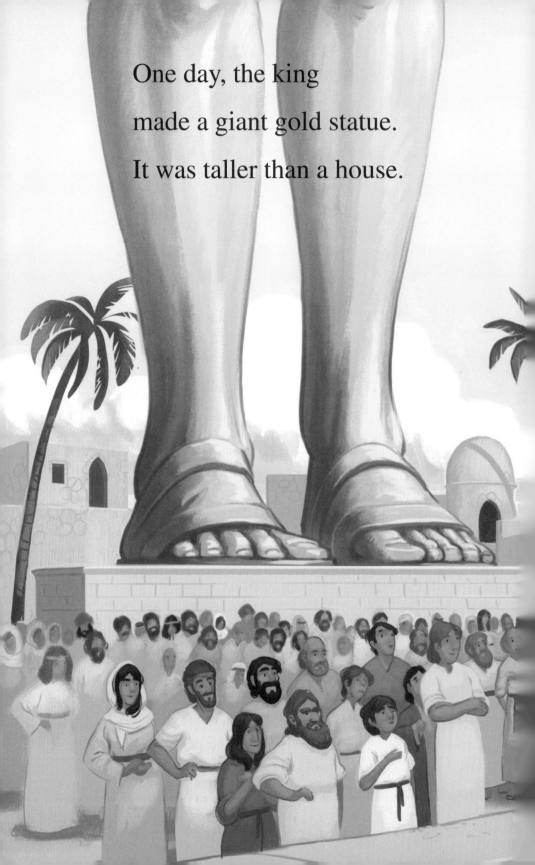

One day, the king
made a giant gold statue.
It was taller than a house.

Nebuchadnezzar told the people,

"You must obey me.

When you hear the sound of music,

you must fall down and worship the statue.

If you don't, you will be thrown

into a blazing furnace!"

The people had to listen.

Nebuchadnezzar was the king.

When they heard the music,

they worshiped the gold statue.

But Shadrach, Meshach, and
Abednego refused to bow down.
They said, "We only worship God."

Nebuchadnezzar was very angry.

He said, "Did you forget?

I will throw anyone who does not obey

me into a blazing furnace!"

18

But the three men said,

"If you throw us into the furnace,

God is able to save us.

But even if he does not,

we still will not worship your statue."

Then King Nebuchadnezzar

was even more angry.

He ordered the furnace

to be seven times hotter than usual.

Soldiers tied up the young men. Shadrach, Meshach, and Abednego were thrown into the blazing furnace.

The king looked into the fire.

Then he jumped to his feet.

He said to his worker,

"Didn't we throw three men in the fire?"

His worker said, "Yes."

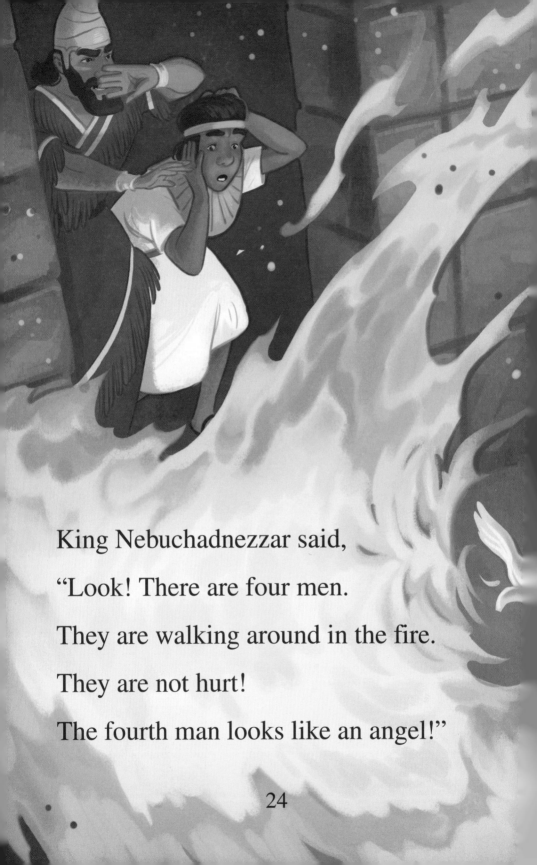

King Nebuchadnezzar said,

"Look! There are four men.

They are walking around in the fire.

They are not hurt!

The fourth man looks like an angel!"

The king walked up to the furnace.

He shouted, "Shadrach, Meshach, and Abednego!

You are servants of the true God!

Come out of there!"

The men walked

out of the furnace.

They were not burned.

They did not even smell like fire.

The king and his servants were amazed!

How could this be?

Then King Nebuchadnezzar said,

"Praise be to the God

of Shadrach, Meshach, and Abednego!

God sent an angel and rescued them."

It was a happy day for the Jews.
Nebuchadnezzar changed his mind.
He said people didn't have to
worship the statue anymore.

They were to worship the true God,

the God of Shadrach, Meshach,

and Abednego.

People in Bible Times

Then Nebuchadnezzar said,
"Praise be to the God of Shadrach, Meshach and Abednego,
who has sent his angel and rescued his servants! They trusted in him and
defied the king's command and were willing to give up their lives rather than serve
or worship any god except their own God."
— *Daniel 3:28*

King Nebuchadnezzar

We pronounce the King's name as: neb-u-kad-nez'-ar

King Nebuchadnezzar was the king of Babylon. He was their king from 605–562 BC
and is most famous for capturing Jerusalem. He is featured in the Book of Daniel
and is mentioned in several other books of the Old Testament.

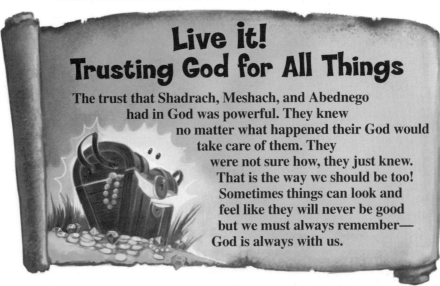

Live it!
Trusting God for All Things

The trust that Shadrach, Meshach, and Abednego
had in God was powerful. They knew
no matter what happened their God would
take care of them. They
were not sure how, they just knew.
That is the way we should be too!
Sometimes things can look and
feel like they will never be good
but we must always remember—
God is always with us.